Advance Praise

AS A CERTIFIED life and business coach, I see the impacts of poor control over money each and every day. I have experienced first hand how the very idea of "money management" can immobilize people. I have seen exactly how that silly green stuff can be horribly intimidating, even in an inanimate form! Money creates critical problems with which far too many Americans have difficulty, for which there is a growing number of books addressing the topic. Crystal Gifford's book, however, stands out in the crowd. It is a wealth of wisdom and knowledge, and is the perfect combination of tools, tips and step-by-step choices to make personal life and financial change. She has put great effort into putting complex financial ideas into simple, understandable language.

The Money Makeover is a wonderful guide to managing your money with simple strategies that don't overwhelm. Her down to earth writing style takes you through a process that helps change your outlook on how to control, spend, invest and save money. Her tips to maintain a strong budget begin with key points on how to get out of debt. Putting her passion into print is most certainly a counter to a financial crisis that has lead far too many to experience serious money issues.

~ **Anna Weber** | BSBM, MAOM, CLC
4-Dimensional Success

THERE IS LITTLE doubt debt has the capacity to cripple not only individuals, but our nation as a whole. Until we understand the possible solutions and are encouraged to take directed action - it is more than likely we will remain stuck with the dark burden of debt overload.

The Money Makeover offers specific, doable solutions to your debt questions and challenges. I applied the principles that Dr. Gifford shares and they are working incredibly well. Crystal offers "a few adjustments to how you handle debt" which relieved my increasing levels of fear and procrastination... because her plan was manageable. This book also helped reduce my stress with a powerful and positive forward-focused action plan. I can now focus on what matters in my personal and business money management, and my clients also now enjoy the benefit of Crystal's wisdom.

~ **Dr. Dianne A. Allen**, Ambassador to the Gifted and Talented
Visions Applied

The Money Makeover

*How to Easily Get Out of Debt,
Create Wealth, and
Leverage Passive Income*

By:

Dr. Crystal Dawn Gifford, CFP®

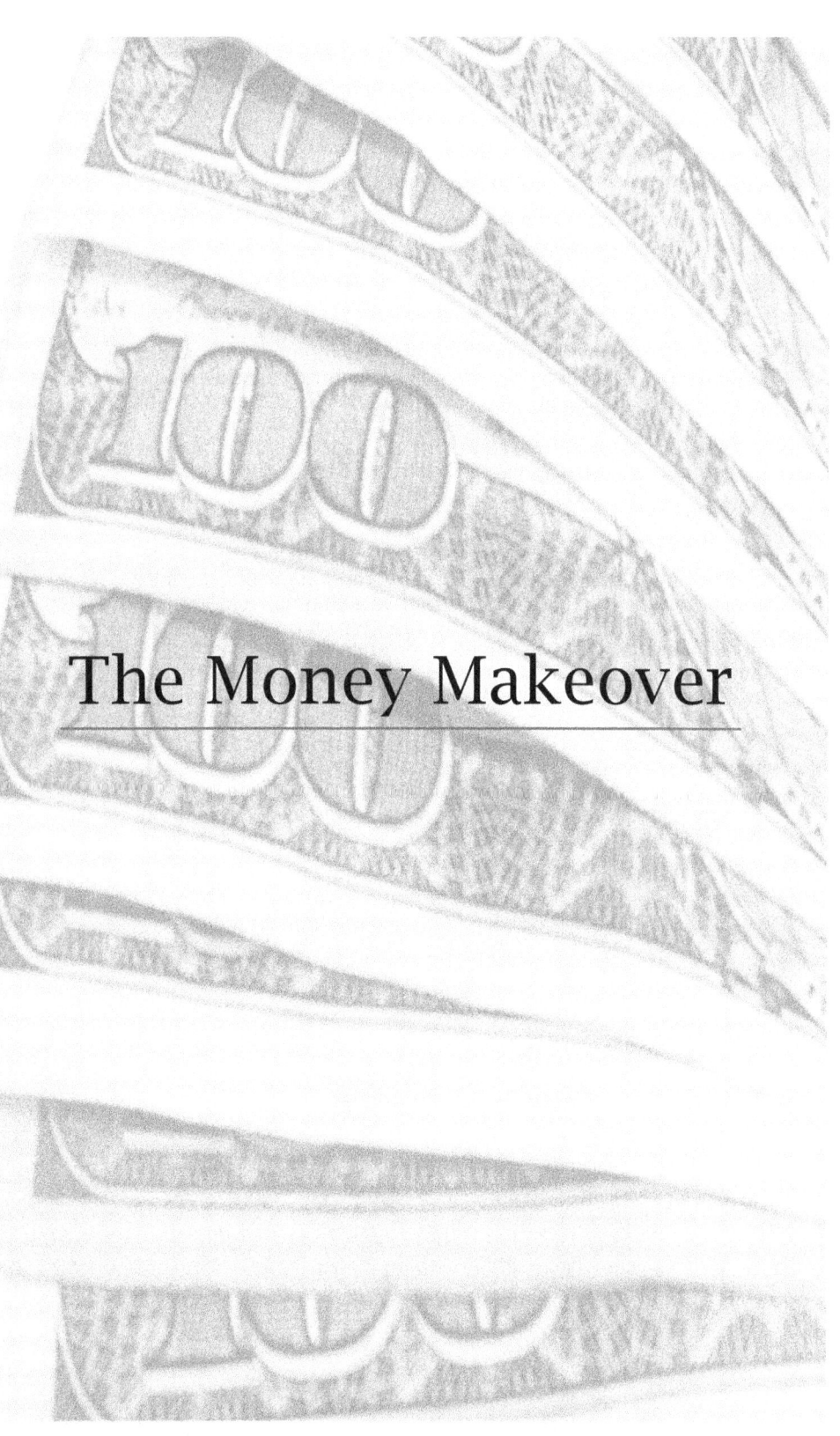

The Money Makeover

Copyright © 2012, ©2015 Empowered Wealthy Woman

ISBN-13: 978-0996297202
ISBN-10: 0996297200

Kindle ASIN: B00C3HKMUQ

No part of this publication may be reproduced, stored in a retrieval system, or transmitted in any form by any means, electronic, mechanical, photocopying, recording, scanning or otherwise, except as permitted under Section 107 or 108 of the 1976 United States Copyright Act, without either the prior written permission of the Publisher, or authorization through payment of the appropriate per-copy fee to the Copyright Clearance Center, Inc., 222 Rosewood Drive, Danvers, MA 01923, (978) 750-8400, or on the Internet at http://www.copyright.com.

Limit of Liability/Disclaimer of Warranty: While the Publisher and author have used their best efforts in preparing this book, they make no representations or warranties with respect to the accuracy or completeness of the contents of this book and specifically disclaim any implied warranties of merchantability or fitness for a particular purpose. No warranty may be created or extended by sales representatives, or written sales materials. The advice and strategies contained herein may not be appropriate for your particular purpose. The publisher is not engaged in rendering professional services, and you should consult with a professional where appropriate. Neither the publisher nor author shall be liable for any loss of profit or commercial damages, including but not limited to special, incidental, consequential, or other damages.

Empowered Wealthy Woman also publishes books in a variety of electronic formats. Some content that appears in print may not be available in electronic books. For more information about Empowered Wealthy Woman, and its products and services contact:

Customer Support
204 37th Ave N #478
St. Petersburg, FL 33704

Published in the United States of America

10 9 8 7 6 5 4 3 2

Dedication

I DEDICATE THIS book to my two wonderful boys who continue to be the motivating force in my life to be all I can be. I adore you Andrew and Brayden for the wonderful men you are growing up to be and I thank you, for your very presence on this earth pushes me to be more than I ever thought I could be. Everything I do... I do it for you. I love you.

Table of Contents

Advance Praise i
Dedication vii
Foreword xi
Acknowledgements xv
Introduction xvii

My Philosophy on Money 3
   Problems with Debt 7
   Why Are You In Debt? 11

The Good Stuff 19

Method 1
The Snowball Method 21

Method 2
Weigh it Against Your Goals 29

Method 3
Pay It Back Twice 33

Method 4
Refinancing 35

Method 5
Release Yourself From Social Pressures 41
     Shifting the Game 47

Method 6

Build Passive Income for Debt Repayment.................49

Method 7
Work a Few Extra Hours Each Month 61
    Ideas for extra income:..63

Method 8
Focus on The Percentage 65

Method 9
Find Free Money..73

Your Next Step
Automate Your Finances 79

Follow Through
Work Your Plan 89

Using the Steps!
    Steps to Using the Methods: 93

Why Debt Can Be Wonderful 95

References 102

About the Author..103
Crystal Offers Solutions to: 107
Other Books By Dr. Gifford 109

Foreword

PICK UP, READ and follow the guidance in this book – it can change your life forever!

Dr. Crystal Gifford has a unique talent to present powerful and compelling ideas in a manner that is understandable and comprehensive. After meeting Crystal, I saw in her the passion and commitment to help others free themselves of debt and ultimately build wealth for themselves. There is no need to struggle; Crystal provides the key to success in these pages.

Debt is a word and a concept all too common in our society. So much so that many people think it is a normal part of being alive. What is good debt? What is bad debt? How do you become free of financial struggles? All these important aspects are featured in *The Money Makeover.* You do not have to be part of the masses, living in fear and constant stress about financial decisions, teetering often on the brink of major loss. There is another way to live. It is Crystal's passion and intention to write and teach about wealth and building a wealth strategy. It is time to wake up and leave your debt mindset behind. Becoming free of debt is a vital part of your wealth building strategy and the author astutely engages you in viable solutions.

I was first introduced to Dr. Gifford during one of my seminars several years ago. Her focus, dedication and desire to help others were immediately evident. Being interested in her talent, I am happy to support her work in helping you learn and apply these money strategies. As co-founder of the Enlightened Wealth Institute and author of New York Times bestsellers *Creating Wealth, Multiple Streams of Income, Cracking the Millionaire Code* and *The One Minute Millionaire,* my own financial expertise is extensive and my career spans many areas of wealth building. In my experience, there are many ways to approach and solve financial issues and Crystal offers sound information for your benefit and eventual success.

You wonder, "Can I be free of debt and can this plan work for me?" Yes, you can, and yes, the plan can! Crystal's expertise affords her the perfect opportunity to share easy to follow, clear directions. She is committed to walking with you as you free yourself from debt and, over time, become financially free. There is no quick fix. Even an inheritance or large gift of some sort has been statically proven to inflate the problems for most people. The change must first happen inside you. With your focus and commitment and Crystal's direction, you are sure to experience a freedom you may not have felt before. Believe me, financial freedom is worth the sacrifice, focus and patience. When Crystal shared *The Money Makeover* with me, I was impressed by the reader friendly delivery of information that for many is emotionally charged. If you are overwhelmed and confused about what actions to take for real, viable results; look no further. In a meaningful manner, Crystal powerfully addresses debt, how to overcome the problem of debt to eradicate its symptoms, and even how to exploit the upside of certain types of debt. After helping you understand debt and how to begin to have a solid plan, Crystal helps you change your game: to help you focus, shift to being debt free, and literally expand your wealth. Keep an open mind; you may not believe it possible to not only be debt free but also to have wealth; however, it is possible to turn the tide for you with self-honesty, determination, focus and action.

The Money Makeover is a clear and concise wealth guide in which Dr. Gifford makes understandable the many ways to eliminate debt in a systematic and effective manner. No more overwhelm. She walks you through—step by step—the thinking and the strategies to help you become free from the burden of financial woes.

You will have the opportunity to complete questionnaires, which help you gain clarity about viable and powerful solutions for your money challenges. By not only reading, but also completing the questions, you will experience tangible and effective strategies to successfully reduce your debt. You will feel the stress melt away as you read and begin to focus on the perfect answer for your financial circumstances. Crystal also shares real life stories and time proven methods that she used personally, as well as those successful for her clients. Her years of expertise are evident as you read; her resources priceless.

From examining the problem of debt—to reduce and eliminate it—to how to use automation in your favor, Dr. Gifford is spot-on in her presentation. This read is manageable and in a language that will not add anxiety to your already stressful situation. Imagine having a custom solution to help you become free of the financial burden you carry. It is possible. Crystal walks you through the solution; you have only to follow directions and stick to it!

Acknowledgements

THERE ARE SO many people I could acknowledge.

There are so many professors in my journey who inspired me, so many in my business path who have urged me on when I wanted to lie down and quit, and so many colleagues who have made the journey to success so much brighter. I thank you all for your contribution, It would take several pages to name you all, so while you may not see your name, you know you are considered here.

As I prepared for and wrote this book, I was inspired by my mentor Lisa Sasevich and the huge community of Sassies to pull out the best of me and to go boldly into my calling. For that, I am grateful. In my decision to take on this venture, I must thank my always encouraging friend, Lisa Salyers, for her constant love and support even when it seemed I was doing way too much at once. Thank you for the shots of patron and the last minute runs to "B-dubs" to let my mind rest when I hit a wall and needed a moment to refresh my brain.

Also, thank you to my ex-husband, for without your self-serving nature after our divorce, I would not have ended up so deeply in debt, or know what it is like and to need to share this message with the world. God made us who we are for a reason and you have served a powerful purpose in driving me forward in my life. Although our lives and our thought processes are different, I am thankful for the role you have played in my life and for the two beautiful boys who are my world and keep me going when nothing else would have.

As I revise this book to create Version II, I want to add a special thank you to all those who have come into my life in my short time since I moved to Florida. I never knew I could move to a new town where I knew no one and have so many true friends in such a short time. Thank you for encouraging me to stop seeing this book as an insignificant project I did a long time ago and pulling it out to allow it to reach those who really need it. I am blessed to have all of you in my life. This new version is coming to life because of you.

Introduction

DROWNING IN DEBT is not fun. I know this because I have been there. There was a day only a few years ago when I looked at my financial picture and it literally made me stressed and nauseated. I had gone through a separation and was getting divorced and the promises made verbally were not kept, so I had been living on $400/month and my good name for months.

Just over a year after this started, I looked at what I was facing, thousands of dollars in credit card debt, almost $100,000 in student loans, a car loan, and an upcoming need to find a place to live to move out of my ex's family's apartment. On top of all this, I still needed to support my two boys, buy school clothes, get them in sports, and "do what all good parents do" to deal with guilt—spoil them so the suffering from the divorce would be less traumatic.

I finished my terminal degree and started working about 13.5 months later and got my first paycheck about 15 months after the separation began. I immediately got a place to live with my boys and began what I called "operation get out of debt." It took me a couple of months to get in the groove, and I will admit, it was another six months before I truly committed to the actions to reduce the debt I had accumulated.

It was a heavy feeling, and I remember all too well the feeling of shame: *Here I am; a college professor of finance and a practicing financial expert, yet I am deeply in debt!* However, once I finally was able to get my mind focused on the possibility that getting out of debt was possible, I began to act accordingly.

I spent the next twelve months using the strategies I share with you in this book—to reduce my debt, and doing so on a teacher's salary, plus my other side business work. I managed to reduce my debt by $36,000 in only 12 months and be free of credit card debt. I want you to understand, however, that this was a full twelve months of pure dedication and discipline. I was on a mission.

In order to follow these tips and reach your financial goals successfully, you must also be fully committed in heart, mind, and action. What kept me going during this time was the vision I had for myself of a better life. This was a life of freedom and financial abundance. In this vision life, I was able to make decisions based on what was best for me instead of the balance available on my credit cards.

I held this vision close as I made each decision, spent some long nights working, and sent each check to pay another chunk toward reducing debt and welcoming freedom into my life. I share this with you to invite you to find the vision that supports and motivates you to do whatever is necessary to reach your goals. It is my wish this book empowers you to take the steps—one day at a time—toward your own financial freedom. May you be blessed and live abundantly.

The Money Makeover

How to Easily Get Out of Debt, Create Wealth, and Leverage Passive Income

My Philosophy on Money

THERE ARE MANY financial gurus out there who tout money solutions and offer you fancy schemes to get rich and reduce debt. While there actually are some amazing strategies and solid solutions, there are just as many options out there that effectively create cash flow for the creator of the products, but deliver very little value to the market.

I am here to tell you honestly that you will not find fancy strategies in this book. It is a book to incorporate real strategies based on unfailing principles. Following these strategies will take work and dedication, just like losing weight in a sustainable way takes basic principles of diet and exercise. I will not promise you that **reading** this book will change your life. What I will promise is if you **apply** the strategies in this book diligently and faithfully, you can experience massive transformation in your life.

For just a moment in this busy life, I want to share with you what I consider the real secrets to success, happiness, and wealth. So many believe wealth is all about money. In reality, financial gains are only a small portion of what truly creates wealth.

So many of my clients come to me seeking help with "money." What we find when we get to the core of their desires is how many actually seek happiness, peace, freedom, and the ability to truly live life. What I have discovered is that when we seek money, what we find is the process of chasing it. Unfortunately, the act of chasing after money creates the energy of lack and invites more of the same.

When we seek instead the freedom, the peace, the joy, and the power to live, which are often supported by abundance of money, the money we think we want naturally follows.

The key to truly inviting wealth into our lives is to embrace the many aspects that make up wealth. I call them the Pillars of Wealth™. They include financial, spiritual, mental, emotional, relational, physical, and inter-dimensional pillars, which together establish a full invitation to a life of living full out. I fervently believe life is meant to be lived! When we connect with the Pillars of Wealth and allow ourselves to build the life of which we dream, we create for ourselves an open

My Philosophy on Money

channel of support from the Universe to achieve our goals.

It is important to understand as you read the contents of this book the purpose is not to simply get you out of debt. This book is about improving your standard of living, and creating a lifestyle that supports your desires. When the debt is gone, the income strategies in this book—as well as the income you have freed up from debt payments—offer a new way of living where you are in control and **you** decide what you do, when, with whom, and how much of it.

You already know you should reduce your debt load, but do you know why debt is so harmful to you? Each year American households go thousands of dollars into debt, despite warnings from the media and the plethora of financial advisors who promise to get you out of debt if you buy their products. While others fight to show you the dangers of debt, our government encourages debt, telling you to spend more... to help the flow of money in the economy.

With all this mixed information, it can be confusing what you should really do. We are one of the wealthiest nations in the world, so why are we still swimming in debt? There are many reasons for this; to find and understand them is the key to eliminate debt from your life once and for all.

Now, I want you to understand one thing. Debt is wonderful. "What?" you ask, as your head reels with the suggestion. "How can you write a book on getting out of debt and say debt is wonderful?" Well, as promised, I plan to share with you my secrets to get and stay out of debt. However, in this book of humble truth I will also share with you the many virtues of debt that no one else wants you to know. But first, let's go into the ways debt does not serve you and why you want to eliminate harmful forms of debt before you address how to use it to work for you.

Problems with Debt

THERE ARE MANY reasons why debt is considered ugly and evil in modern day America, and they are good ones. Often, families, individuals, college students, and others find themselves in debt and do not even know how they got there. Even business professionals all over the U.S. have come forward to admit their debt load is a burden, in spite of their tremendous successes in business.

So if everyone is in debt, what is the big deal? Why do we worry about eliminating debt in a society that thrives on borrowed funds? There are many reasons to eliminate debt, and if you are reading this book you likely have experienced some of them yourself.

> **Debt can create a sense of overwhelm and hinders productivity in your business, your work, your social life, and your health.**
>
> ~ Crystal Cooley Gifford

If you have ever tried to accomplish a task that you just cannot seem to finish, it is likely due to the looming sense of overwhelm; your debt can play a significant role in the trapped energy that does not allow you to progress. But don't worry, we are going to reveal how to set in motion a plan that will reduce or even eliminate any sense of overwhelm even before you actually get the debt paid off.

Another dilemma with debt is that many professional people who find themselves in debt are often much too ashamed to admit they have a problem and seek help. Too often, professionals strive to just make more money to try to use it to eliminate the debt, but the more money they make the more debt they attract. Why is this?

You must remove the habits and conditions in your life that created the debt at the lower levels of income before you can ever be successful in eliminating it at the higher income levels.

Embarrassment and shame are often the byproduct of debt, but why does this shame exist? It is so common in our country to have large amounts of debt that it seems, at a glance, trivial to be ashamed of this in your own personal situation. It is not the debt itself that causes the shame, however. Debt screams a loud message to many of a lack of self-control and inability to master a critical area of their lives. When we find ourselves highly in debt, the shame comes from

My Philosophy on Money

the inability to perform in such a crucial area... not from the debt itself.

Yet another issue with debt is the health and mental problems, which arise from the stress and worry of potentially not paying bills on time and loss of reputation or integrity—not to mention the potential public humiliation if the credit score is tarnished. The fear of financial ruin often creates added stressors in the body, which might never be experienced under no-debt circumstances. The inability to pay, or the fear that a dip in income would create an inability to pay, emotionally cripples people all over the world and creates insomnia every night for many across the U.S.

There are other significant and truly financially harmful results of debt that must be included as well.

When you are in debt, one of the first things you will notice is that the true cost of everything increases.

If you try to get another loan to purchase something, the interest rates will be higher for two main reasons. First, your high debt-to-income ratio drives up the interest rate charged you by the lending institution. Second, higher levels of debt, caused by maxed out use of available credit, will lower your credit score... which, again, drives up the interest rate the lending institution charges.

The interest rate is what it costs you (aka the price) of using someone else's money. Therefore, when your interest rate is increased, the price of anything else you purchase when using debt is also increased.

The second financially harmful attribute of high debt is the missed opportunities you face on a regular basis... by having maxed out debt and the inability to pursue these possible options.

Think about how many times you saw an opportunity to get in on a great deal that could have put some real money in your pocket right away... if only you could come up with the cash to jump in on the deal. I call these "debt-quashed missed fortunes," since debt was the one thing that crushed your opportunity to contribute to your financial fortune.

Wouldn't it be great to learn how you can set yourself up to never miss this kind of opportunity again? I thought so. But before we can explore how to eliminate the debt monsters, we must first understand what got you there in the first place.

My Philosophy on Money

Why Are You In Debt?

THERE ARE MANY issues that contribute to rising debt. These are not the same for all people, and you may recognize your own patterns in some of the areas we discuss here as examples. However, one thing evident in all cases of unhealthy debt is the lack of plan and follow-through to accomplish the things you want to accomplish... in a way that best serves you.

One common cause of debt is a simple lack of structure in your spending patterns.

Don't be harsh on yourself; we all have those one or two areas where we could use some improvement. Regardless of how much time and energy you have spent on self-improvement, it is likely you still have at least one area in which you know you could do better. You are not alone in this, and no one expects you to be superhuman. In fact, having minor flaws that need improvement are what keeps us going and contributing to society to help others.

So why is this particular flaw so daunting? It is because this one eats away at the hard earned money you spent time away from your family, friends, and loved ones to earn. The issue here is not that you cannot control your spending, most likely. It is that you intuitively recognize you do not have a system or plan that motivates you and guides you to good spending choices.

We've all seen movies of shop-a-holics, but you do not have to be addicted to shopping to exhibit poor spending habits. In fact, many ordinary, conservative people find themselves every year, looking at their tax returns wondering where all their money went. Poor spending patterns do not always mean lack of control, they simply mean you lack a system to support your goals, but one that instead supports the goals of retailers everywhere. This is consumerism at its finest and we all can easily fall prey every day of our lives. If this possible transformation is for you… a few tweaks later in this book, and we will have you on your way to financial freedom.

Another common reason for high debt levels is to keep up with a social status in which you may find yourself living.

Far too often, it is the very people who would normally be comfortable living a modest lifestyle that find themselves spending much more than they ever dreamed they would or could as their income levels rise. They feel a sense of social pressure to perform like, look like, and smell like the proverbial "Joneses." Often this pressure

My Philosophy on Money

begins to build long before income levels can actually support this level of spending, and therefore the debt pattern begins long before it is recognizable.

The social pressure, mostly self-induced by association, takes form as another money monster that controls financial decisions both spontaneously and in planned purchases. If social status pressure is the cause of your debt problem, then you must first assess how real that pressure is, what its source is, and whether it serves you to your highest good. This issue will be addressed in detail later in this book.

Another major way people sometimes find themselves in debt is due to failed ventures.

You may have been a risk-taker in an earlier part of your life, or maybe you still are, and you have accumulated mounds of debt from ventures that did not fare so well. Sadly, this type of debt usually comes with the highest debt levels and the highest stress levels as a sense of failure may also be associated with it, and serve as a constant reminder of the failed attempt to rise above your old circumstances. This type of debt typically assumes the heaviest weight on the emotional and physical stresses associated with debt and can also create blocks in other areas of your life.

If this is your reason for high debt and you feel absolutely hopeless, I have good news for you. This is usually the easiest type of debt to eliminate since it is not associated with patterns that must first be broken. Consider this type of debt a broken pencil that you simply need to sharpen so you can get back out there again and make life happen. You are a go-getter and if you got into debt under these circumstances, it is likely you will work just as diligently to get out of debt and achieve your dreams after all. A few adjustments to the way you are approaching the debt and you will be well on your way to debt-free living.

Pause and Reflect

Take a moment to think about how you have accumulated the debt you currently have. It may be one way, or multiple ways. Be honest with yourself and allow the truth to show up for you. This will help you identify and change the patterns that got you here. As said by Einstein and paraphrased here, "The thinking that got you here cannot be the same thinking that gets you there." Let's change this pattern; it starts with getting clear on how you got here.

As you pause and reflect, take time to respond to the questions that follow. To read them is to develop one level of awareness; to actually take time to answer them takes you to a deeper place within where you acknowledge feelings you have simply quashed, actions of which you were not aware, and dreams you let die on the vine.

The Money Makeover

What items, experiences, intended investments or other goods were purchased that led to my debt?

_____
_____
_____
_____
_____
_____
_____
_____
_____
_____

How necessary were the items, goods, intended investments or experiences that led to debt?

_____
_____
_____
_____
_____
_____
_____
_____
_____
_____

My Philosophy on Money

Am I still purchasing more of these items, goods, intended investments, or experiences?

_____
_____
_____
_____
_____
_____
_____
_____

What about these purchases has made my life better?

_____
_____
_____
_____
_____
_____
_____
_____
_____
_____

The Money Makeover

What about these purchases feel wasted to me?

_____
_____
_____
_____
_____
_____
_____
_____
_____

What am I going to change about these spending patterns moving forward?

_____
_____
_____
_____
_____
_____
_____
_____
_____
_____
_____

The Good Stuff

How to Stop the Debt Trap and Dig Your Way Out

NOW THAT YOU have worked through why you accumulated large amounts of debt, let's spend some time with the reason you are reading this book—how to now eliminate debt from your life. In this section I discuss what I consider the top nine methods, which will help eliminate debt from your life. This is not a "quick fix" or "fad diet" type of money mastery method. These methods are tried and true and have worked for thousands all over the U.S. to eliminate debt and keep it at bay for good.

Warning! You will not be applying all of these methods at the same time, or your head may explode (just kidding, but you don't want to create a system that is too unreasonable to follow). So let's get started on your way to the multitude of ways you can eliminate debt.

The Money Makeover

Here we go…

Method 1

The Snowball Method

THERE ARE COMMON debt reduction practices taught in all our credit counseling agencies and by paid advisors all over the U.S. If you apply this system diligently, you are sure to become debt free. Once you understand the system, it is quite easy to follow. The trick to this one, however, is sticking with the plan.

You will find your disposable income (that is the income left over after you have paid all of your obligations) will continue to increase as you progress through this plan, so it is critical to keep your eyes on the end prize—a debt-free life—in order for this one to work. Let's go through the Snowball Method and then look at an example so you can confidently apply it to your personal money mastery journey.

I strongly suggest you make this one of your primary methods as you choose which to apply first; this one works like magic if you only stick to it. I personally used this method to eliminate

The Money Makeover

$36,000 of credit card and other debt within 12 months during my first year back to working full time after a painful divorce.

The snowball method is about building up your disposable income as you eliminate debt and then apply the additional disposable income to the next debt until it is paid off, freeing up even more disposable income that you can apply to the next debt… and so on. Sounds confusing? The following will show you exactly what you need to do to apply this example.

Warning! The Snowball Method requires you first create a budget to determine what your current disposable income is. A warning, perhaps, but no worries! In the next section I will show you how you can get help with the budget process and help you deal with whatever negative emotions the word **budget** brings up for you.

Example: The Snowball Method

Let's assume we are working with your good friend, Linda, to eliminate debt. Linda is a successful businesswoman bringing in a very healthy income but has found herself deeply in debt.

The Snowball Method

After working on her budget to include all necessary expenses for housing, transportation, business travel, and other expenses, even leaving room to enjoy her occasional treat to herself for working hard, Linda found she had an additional $500 per month she could apply to her debt payments. This was after all of her debt payments were paid for the month as well. Linda wrote down all of her debt payments, balances, and interest rates as in the following chart:

Mortgage	$180,000	6%	$260,000	$1800
Car Note	$17,000	8%	$20,000	$420
Visa	$8,000	15%	$0	$220
Master Card	$12,000	17%	$0	$300
Best Buy	$4000	25%	$800	$60
Nordstrom	$1200	25%	$0	$40
Apple, Inc.	$3500	18%	$2000	$120
Student Loans	$45,000	4%	No paper value	$500
Personal Line	$20,000	10%	$0	$800

Looking at her debt in this perspective, Linda felt overwhelmed and had decided that even with her income in the top percentage of female income earners in the US, she may never get out of debt. Imagine also that you have just come back from a conference with The Empowered Wealth Network and you have a rock solid plan to help Linda get out of debt.

What would your advice to Linda be? Let's run through the scenario of how Linda will approach this debt until it is paid.

First, you want to realign the debt in the order of the interest rates so it is easy to determine which to pay first.

In most cases, you will always want to focus on eliminating the debt with the highest interest rate first.

Occasionally, you may find a debt with a lower rate, but a small balance, in which case you may choose to eliminate it first to create a sense of accomplishment to fuel your success as you progress. Otherwise, always focus on the highest interest rate first. Please keep in mind any additional fees should be considered when determining which of the interest rates is higher.

Upon reevaluation, Linda's debt in order of interest rate looks like the figures in the following chart:

The Snowball Method

Type of Debt	Account Balance	Interest Rate	Value of asset tied to debt	Monthly Debt Payment
Nordstrom	$1200	25%	$0	$40
Best Buy	$4000	25%	$800	$60
Apple, Inc.	$3500	18%	$2000	$120
Master Card	$12,000	17%	$0	$300
Visa	$8,000	15%	$0	$220
Personal Line	$20,000	10%	$0	$800
Car Note	$17,000	8%	$20,000	$420
Mortgage	$180,000	6%	$290,000	$1800
Student Loans	$45,000	4%	No paper value	$500

Now that we have rearranged her debt by interest rate, we can easily look at which debts are costing the most to keep and which are the least expensive. Using the Snowball Method is now as easy as choosing the debt with the highest cost and putting all of your resources to eliminating that one first.

Since we know that Linda has an extra $500 she is able and willing to apply toward reducing debt, our advice to Linda is to pay the full $500 plus the $40 she is currently paying so the monthly amount paid to Nordstrom (the 25%

interest rate) is $540. She has chosen the Nordstrom account first because it has the highest interest rate.

You can see that during the third month, the Nordstrom balance would be eliminated and the extra money that month can be paid toward Best Buy. Starting with the fourth month, the Best Buy payment made will be $600. This comes from the $60 existing payment already in the budget plus the $540 Linda has freed up by paying off Nordstrom.

The values will accumulate like this and the payments will grow larger as each debt it repaid. Once Best Buy is paid in just over six months, the payment for Apple will go to $720, followed by the payment to the Master Card of $1020, then to Visa of $1240, and the personal line of credit will jump to $2040 once all the other balances are paid. All this has occurred without the need for Linda to stretch her budget and continually downgrade her lifestyle.

The original application of $500 from the budget toward debt reduction has allowed this process to begin. Now, once Linda has paid of the car note with the final payment of $2460, she can decide if it is in her best interest for tax purposes to continue the process to pay off the mortgage and the student loans. Since these rates are 6% and 4% respectively, it may benefit more for Linda to begin investing this $2460 per month toward building wealth at a higher rate of return than she pays (on an after tax basis) for the mortgage and student loans.

Note: If you are interested in the breakdown of exactly how much interest would be saved by this method compared to continually paying minimum payments or if you want to know exactly how long it should take to be debt free, enter your information in the Contact Us section on our website. We've made it easy to go online at www.crystalgifford.com to check out our book resources, and take advantage of an opportunity to receive assessment templates to easily input your own information and quickly get results.

***

Pause and Reflect

List your debts in the following chart, including type, interest rates, balances, and monthly payments then rank them in order of highest interest rate first.

The Money Makeover

Rank #1 Highest interest rate	Type of Debt	Account Balance	Interest Rate	Value of asset tied to debt	Monthly Debt Payment

Method 2

Weigh it Against Your Goals

ONE OF THE most effective ways I was able to avoid going deeper into debt while I was paying down my debt a few years ago was to make a conscious choice with each purchase. I do not believe it is healthy to live on a budget that is so restrictive you feel like you can never reward yourself.

So, for those of you who want to tap into budgeting—while feeling great about the process instead of constrained (more on this mindset later)—I have great news. You can easily begin to reduce your spending with a method I call weighing each purchase against your goals.

I want you to go with me for a moment into this next scenario. Imagine you are shopping at a department store and the most amazing jacket is on the rack calling your name (jackets and trendy coats are one of my weaknesses). You have fallen in love with this jacket and you really want to buy it, but you know you do not have the cash, so you think about putting it on your credit card. As your financial advisor, I would encourage you, if you really want it... buy that jacket!

However, before you make the purchase, let's go on a quick journey in your mind. Imagine yourself three months into the future, six months, one year. How important will that jacket be to you in these future moments? Do you believe there will be something in your life that is enhanced by that jacket? If you cannot see a clear way in which that jacket will have made your life truly better beyond this moment in the store, then this is a clear "walk away" transaction. Don't buy it. However, if you can honestly see how it may have a positive effect, such as higher self-esteem, landing a business deal, or an employment opportunity, you owe it to yourself to take the time to weigh that positive effect **agains**t an alternative empowering positive effect—reaching your monetary goals.

Let's say, for instance, that the jacket will cost you $100. It seems like such a small amount, but when you apply the interest on that $100 over the next five years that you may be paying off your debt, you will find that at the high interest rates

Weigh it Against Your Goals

paid, that $100 will cost you $305! When you weigh that cost and recognize that this will put you behind on your goal of getting out of debt by almost a month, if the jacket is still worth it to you and the benefits you foresee from your honest assessment are greater, you should consider buying it.

I used this method to walk away from many purchases during my debt reduction process, and it worked to help me reach my goal more quickly than I had imagined. More importantly, I walked away from those purchases with a sense of pride and fulfillment rather than feeling cheated or constrained. I actually left the mall feeling like I bought exactly what I wanted... a shorter time until I was debt free. It was very empowering.

Pause and Reflect

Write down your goals. What is so important to you that you MUST achieve it in the next 12-18 months? List any financial goals here. Whenever making a purchase decision, ask yourself if that decision moves you toward your goal or away from it. If it moves you toward your goal, it may

The Money Makeover

be a good decision. If it moves you away from your goal, ask yourself, "Is this worth delaying my objective?"

Goal List your goal here	Price or Cost of Goal in dollars and/or months	Level of Importance 1=not important 10=very important	Notes to remember about goal when making purchase
1.			
2.			
3.			
4.			
5.			
6.			
7.			
8.			
9.			
10.			

Method 3

Pay It Back Twice

THE THIRD EMPOWERING method for getting out of debt is creating a system for use of your credit accounts so you use them for your regular payments and budget in enough free cash flow to pay back on the charge accounts twice the amount you charge. This one can be tricky because it requires you to carefully examine your purchases and be **diligen**t in paying back at least twice the amount you have charged.

This is a very simple method to understand. The difficult part is implementation. All you do is look at your purchases each month and send a payment to your charge accounts for exactly twice what you purchased. Over time, you will reach a point where there is no balance left and you can just use the card and pay it off each month. If you have other types of debt (installment payments, for instance), the extra money you are no longer using to pay back twice your purchases for the month can be applied to those to continue the debt reduction using the snowball method.

Pause and Reflect

Take a moment to write out a plan for how you will address the pay-back twice method. Perhaps you have a certain card you want to focus on paying off first. Write down your plan here, and as you begin to make purchases, gather up the funds from those purchases to send a payment monthly, weekly, or even daily to that card you wish to pay off. Write your plan here.

_____
_____
_____
_____
_____
_____
_____
_____
_____
_____
_____
_____
_____
_____

Method 4

Refinancing

ONE OF THE most commonly used methods of reducing debt payments in the United States is refinancing a mortgage. After the mortgage and banking crisis in 2008, this method no longer works for everyone, due to low property values and high mortgage balances. However, this is still a viable method for you if you have remaining equity in your home and a good credit rating.

Before I offer the usefulness of this method, let me first give the important warning that if you refinance your home to consolidate debt and you run the debt back up, it will be much more difficult to get out of debt in the future.

Two of the biggest drawbacks of refinancing your home are: how easy it feels, and how frequently consumers find themselves spending to their maximum capacity again plus... they are also the not-so-proud owners of a higher mortgage. Do not let this be **your** mistake! You must also remember that if you move debt from unsecured to secured, you are now risking your secured asset in place of payment, should you not be able to pay.

Now, let's move on to the wonderful world of refinance and debt consolidation. One of the primary reasons consolidation helps reduce debt is because all of your high interest rate debt is now placed into a lower one. Mortgages are secured by your home, so rates are considerably lower. If you refinance and pay only the minimum mortgage payment, you will not get out of debt much faster than you would have using any of the other methods previously mentioned.

The most important thing to understand if you refinance: in order to reduce debt, the process of reduction actually begins **after** you have signed the contract. You have likely incurred some fees during the new contract, so you have increased your debt slightly unless you paid these fees in cash. Once you determine refinancing is a good choice for you and you have completed the process, only then does debt reduction begin.

You want to take all of the debt payments you were making prior to the refinance and continue to pay this amount toward your mortgage each month. Let's use Linda as an example. Her total monthly debt is $4260 (or $3760 ignoring her

Refinancing

student loans). If Linda would refinance her home for the $245,700 needed to pay all debt except student loans, her new payment would be about $1473 per month with a 30-year mortgage at 6%.

This new, lower payment would free up around $2287 per month. Keep in mind, however, if Linda were ten years into her mortgage, she effectively just increased the amount of time until the mortgage is paid in full. If, however, Linda applies the full payment of $3760 toward the mortgage each month, the full balance would be paid off in less than seven years. If Linda still could afford the additional $500 used in the snowball method, these two method combined could have her out of debt in no time.

Note: At the time of this writing, mortgage rates are again at all-time lows. You will want to check the current market rates and create a full analysis of whether this is right and a possible choice for you given your financial specifics. There are typically fees and loan-to-value limits involved with new mortgage contracts, so you must determine whether this ultimately is the best move for you financially. You can contact one of our financial analysts for a strategy session concerning this analysis by entering your request and contact information at www.yescrystal.com.

The Money Makeover

Pause and Reflect

Refinancing your home can be a little scary if you don't fully understand the process. Before you begin, call at least three local lending institutions and ask the how their process works, what are their current interest rates, payback terms, and other relevant information. Do your research and find the loan that works best for you. A lender who will allow you to pay on a weekly or biweekly basis offers a ton of added value. Use this area to take notes on what you have learned as you inquire at each lender.

<u>Lender 1</u>

_____
_____
_____
_____
_____
_____
_____
_____
_____
_____
_____
_____

Refinancing

Lender 2
_____

Lender 3
_____

Method 5

Release Yourself From Social Pressures

THERE ARE MANY pressures that have likely brought you to this place of being burdened by high debt. For some, it was a series of events that took you beyond your resources, a failed business, divorce, or some other reasons. But for some of you, the debt is primarily consumer-driven and it is highly a part of your attempts to keep up with society and keep up a certain appearance.

While this desire to appear successful may have its strong points, such as landing a business deal by wearing professional clothes, there are very few industries where the type of car you drive or the clothes you wear must be to a certain standard rather than simply portray a specific style. A business meeting in a suit is just as wonderful regardless of brand.

Now before you argue this is not true in your industry, I will recognize that if you are in the fashion industry it may be necessary for you to maintain a certain wardrobe or if you are a stock broker, financial advisor, real estate agent, or some other type of public service agent who may need to drive clients around in a high-ticket vehicle. The trick is to recognize the **why** of such potential luxury purchases and stick with only those that support your business.

Once you have identified which expenditures truly support your business, you can begin to eliminate some others you have perhaps acquired through habit. This method of debt management or reduction will require some soul searching and an honest look at what brought on the debt, as discussed earlier. You will need to align your goal of getting out of debt with your behavior and need for material items.

Using a method, which loudly calls you to release yourself from social pressure, we do not suggest you eliminate all luxury purchases or feel deprived, but simply reevaluate all purchases for the future and determine if they lead you toward your goals or away from them.

Release Yourself From Social Pressures

This method is like weight loss. You can apply all the techniques you want and "go for it" again and again... but until you have the mindset to be successful, and add in willpower, determination, and reality checks, your will power can only last so long before old habits resume. The good news is, however, that if you really want to be free of debt, it is very possible to accomplish your goal.

If you are committed to debt reduction, then follow the exercise below to remove yourself from societal pressure to indulge yourself to an unhealthy point of debt, the first step of which is to go through all of your existing "stuff" and see how much of it serves you on a daily, weekly, or even monthly basis. Carefully consider each of the following questions:

How many items remain in your closet with tags still on them?

_____
_____
_____
_____
_____
_____
_____

The Money Makeover

How cluttered is your garage, closet, bedroom, living room, etc?

_____
_____
_____
_____
_____
_____
_____
_____
_____
_____

Do you find yourself overwhelmed with "stuff" that you have no idea when and where you might use?

_____
_____
_____
_____
_____
_____
_____
_____
_____
_____
_____

Release Yourself From Social Pressures

This exercise should reveal just how deeply you may have bought into consumerism, without ever being aware of it.

You must make a mindset shift here before you can move forward. Take inventory of all the merchandise in your home that you have not used in more than six months. For seasonal items such as snow skis, this may be extended to a year.

Next, add up the value of all these items if you were purchasing them new today. This should be about how much they cost you when initially purchased. Then, value these items for what they are worth in today's market. You may need to look on eBay, Amazon or some other source to determine the used prices.

After you have documented the prices, look at the items and determine if they have any intrinsic value to you. Did they come from a family member or someone you cherish? You may want to consider why you are hanging on to any items you no longer use and see if you can set yourself free from them—but that issue is for another book.

Now that you have valued these items, how much debt could you eliminate if you simply sold some or all of them? This may be one way to help you on your way to living debt free. More importantly, consider just how much less debt would you have today had you never purchased them. Ouch! That one stings, I know. If you take this one step further and add on the interest paid on those purchases… well, the effects can be painfully awakening.

This exercise is designed to help you acknowledge the full costs of consumerism and empower you to step into a freedom you have not experienced before. To complete this exercise, you are going to take this list and put it near your credit cards—or whatever mode you use for spending. Keep it close by; to remind you each time you consider a possible luxury purchase.

Next, you are going to release yourself from these items. You can give them away, sell them to apply to your debt, burn them, or whatever you choose, but it is critical that you get rid of any items that no longer serve you. Once you have completed this task, come back to this book and put a big checkmark next to this method.

Shifting the Game

So far we have focused on ways you can reduce your debt: to cut back on your spending, focus on a budget, and apply consistent repayment to the balance of your debt, all through careful money management. Each method is a great start and works for most of the population when properly followed... with consistent dedication.

There are a few people, however, for whom these methods alone are not fast enough to effect the necessary change, and for even more, the kind of method that requires too much sacrifice—the kind of sacrifices not sustainable in the long run. My vision for you, as you go through these methods to reduce debt, is to find the process one filled with both enjoyment and accomplishment. I strongly believe you should enjoy the process of reducing debt and focus on the rewarding experience of taking control and making a move toward your ultimate financial freedom.

This is why the next several debt reduction methods include the focus to add rather than reduce something in your life. The upcoming methods will show you how you can expand your income and grow your capacity to pay off debt— so you can continue to live the life you desire and

The Money Makeover

feel completely free as you make these choices to improve your finances.

If you are feeling really aggressive, you can combine both types of strategies to give your debt a 1-2 knockout in no time! Sound like this fits your style a little more? Then read on...

Method 6

Build Passive Income for Debt Repayment

ONE OF MY favorite "toys" in the world is the game of passive income. I love creating it, helping others create it, and watching the results of it manifest in the lives of my clients. This game can be used to reduce debt as well. The way you play is to find something you love to do and monetize it. Then you are going to leverage that activity, service, or other talent so you can begin earning money with very little effort on your part.

The beauty of building passive income: you can first apply every penny of your extra income to reduce your debt, but once the debt is gone you have an improved lifestyle by the debt payments you reduced… not to mention the passive income you created.

Keep in mind there are many types of investments that yield passive income, but if you are still reading this book it is likely you do not have them, or you would have used them to repay your debt. Do you have passive-yield investments, but are not sure how to determine if you should cash them in to reduce debt? I encourage you to visit us at www.crystalgifford.com and request a consultation so we can assist you in an important decision-making process.

Just how do you create passive income and live a life that offers you all the freedoms you desire, plus a continuous flow of income? Let's use an example below to explain,

---

For this example, we are going to visit the home of your good friend, Javier, who works hard at his corporate job where he has transitioned his way to upper level management in a small firm and has done quite well for himself despite an illness four years ago that kept him out of work for eight months.

Build Passive Income for Debt Repayment

Javier has informed you that he will be leaving his corporate job within six months and moving to his new home in Costa Rica, which he recently purchased for cash. You marvel at his ability to make this move and wonder how he made this happen in the past four years, as you know he was deeply in debt and could barely pay his bills during his extended illness.

Curious, you ask Javier how he is making such a big change and how he has the financial stability and freedom to make the move. With a sly grin on his face, Javier invites you into his home office where he pours you a glass of wine, sits back and begins his story.

"You see, dear friend, about four years ago my whole life was in turmoil. I was severely ill and wasn't sure if I was going to be here to support my family and see my children go to college. As you know, Jeffrey was a senior in high school at the time and Maria was a sophomore."

"While stuck in my bed for over six months after I made a miraculous recovery and left a two-month stay at the hospital, I realized I wanted…no, I realized I **needed** something better to offer my family. My corporate job had me busy all the time and each month we always found it difficult to make ends meet. You've heard the phrase, 'Too much month at the end of the money?' That was our reality every month."

"I made a decision that my family and I deserve more than my working so hard for just one vacation a year and the constant worry that an unexpected expense may come up and we would run out of money. We had a nice lifestyle, but it took every penny we made to maintain it. It was then that I came across some books and concepts that changed my life. I learned about this thing called passive income."

"Now, I didn't have a clue what that meant, but the people who were talking about it seemed to be in a different city, or even a different country every week—living the life I dreamed of—so I decided to pay attention."

Javier, continued, "What I learned is that if you have a talent, any talent, you can turn that into passive income. At first I could not come up with anything that could be passive income for me. I am a corporate manager. How could I make more money on that? So I gave up on the idea because I figured the concept didn't apply to me."

Build Passive Income for Debt Repayment

"Then my grandmother came over to cheer me up since I was still stuck in bed, and we started going through some old photo albums. She kept bragging about how I was always the best dancer in my Salsa classes even since junior high. She asked me if I remember how I paid my way through college teaching fellow students how to dance. Then it hit me... *I love to dance! And other people love it too.*"

"I must admit, I felt like I was bragging at first, but the truth is I am a great dancer and a light of hope sprang forth in me that maybe this was my answer to taking care of my family. Only this time, I was armed with the power of knowledge from the financial lessons I had been studying, and the wisdom of a few added years that allowed me to craft a plan to earn money—teaching people to dance while I simply managed and organized the classes and found the students for the program."

I was inspired by Javier's story, as he continued, "Dancing I know, and managing I know even more, so I married the two talents and researched how I could turn my talents and skills into income. By the time I could go back to work full time, I had researched and planned the whole deal and was about to open my first dance studio in a local gym where I could rent the space and charge entry for the lessons."

Javier shared that at first he thought the studio would be temporary because he knew he could not afford the extra time in the long run to continue teaching people to dance. "But through a series of events, I ended up recording my dance lessons for use in the classes when I was going to be away on business. I hired a young college student to be there to guide the dance students through the videos and be sure they were partnering well."

"What I learned was, that once I recorded my moves and instructions in the video, I did not even need to be present for the dance lessons to continue. Over time, my studios grew to ten across the region and now I do more teaching through YouTube and other online media than I could ever manage in a physical space."

He went on to share how his web-based students use his videos to learn all the basics and prepare for the big events. Then, once a year, they hold a Virtual Salsa club reunion event where students from all over the world show up to

Build Passive Income for Debt Repayment

practice and show off their moves to others who have gone through the program.

"I have a total of 200,000 students who have completed my program and we have around 15,000 and growing show up at the events each year. So how do I make money with this online part, you ask? Well, my students pay $497 for the beginner series and work up to the $9,997 advanced videos. A full year of serious training can take someone from beginner to advanced levels if they are dedicated and work hard. Also, they can buy the complete system with four private 1:1 lessons offered by my dance instructors for $14,997 for the entire year. They also pay $5,000 to attend the live event/workshop that ends with live performances."

He went on to explain more about his videos, "The videos are recorded already, and I have a team of experts who handle questions, administration, event planning, and other aspects of the business. I simply show up each April and host the Virtual Salsa Club Reunion. The rewards financially are amazing, and I no longer need to work the corporate job. I stayed long enough to make sure the company can do well when I leave, but with the income I generate from the Virtual

The Money Makeover

Salsa Club, I can retire to Costa Rica with my wife and still support my children through college."

"To this day, I am so thankful that my grandmother came over with that photo album and inspired me to remember my own talents and abilities while I was in one of the darkest places in my life. If she hadn't come by, and if I hadn't been ready and willing to make the risky investment in myself, I would still be drudging along just to make ends meet. Be open my friend, for you never know when the moment is **now** to make your move. I listened to the whisper, and it has saved me and created a higher quality of life for my family and generations to come."

Dancing may not be your "thing", but what is "your thing"? We all have something. What is it that you are great at doing, love to do, or always seem to be complimented on when you are doing it? Maybe you don't even see it as a gift because it is so simple to you. That is what makes it amazing. It is simple to you, but not to others.

Build Passive Income for Debt Repayment

Pause and Reflect

Stop reading for just a moment and make a list of all those talents, skills, and hobbies you have that seem so simplistic to you. Maybe you receive compliments on them all time. Maybe no one even knows you have this talent because you hide it. Don't worry just yet about how that could be monetized. Just breathe in the acceptance of your gifts and transfer them to paper.

My talents, gifts, and "easy" activities are:

_____
_____
_____
_____
_____
_____
_____
_____
_____
_____
_____
_____
_____
_____

The Money Makeover

Build Passive Income for Debt Repayment

Ok, now that you have written down your talents, keep this list close by, and every time you get an inspiration, write it down. Use extra space, your own notebook, or a digital journal to keep these written down. Don't worry; I am not going to ask you to pursue every one of them, but I do encourage you to choose the one talent or skill that makes you smile with every part of your being—and consider the possibilities of this to create passive (or even extra) income.

If you decide to make a move on this possibility, I would love to hear your story! Please email me the details at crystal@crystalgifford.com with a short summary of your inspired action and what you've done so far to make it happen. However, if you struggle to make the connection between talents, possibilities and income, we also have coaches available to help you work through that inspiration and turn it into an income producing activity.

Maybe you haven't thought of any ideas to make money with your "thing" just yet. We are here to help inspire you. A sample list of areas of your life you could use to create passive income is included below for your convenience.

The Money Makeover

Please note, these are just a few of the multitude of possibilities; limited only by your imagination!

- Monetize your blog.
- Start a membership site.
- Sell a product on the Internet (drop shipping or your own).
- Sell a service on the Internet that you have delegated to others to provide.
- Affiliate Marketing (promote others' products and/or services).
- Create a web-based game or service that charges for added features.
- Create information products and sell them online.
- Create a service website (job searches, dating, etc.).
- Write an e-book on your expertise and promote it to others' lists for profit sharing.
- Build your own list of prospects and offer valuable services for which they will pay.

Method 7

Work a Few Extra Hours Each Month

PERHAPS YOU READ the story above and it didn't capture or compel you. Maybe you are not a risk taker or you are not quite ready yet to dream so big... hang around us for a while and you will be!

For you, maybe the idea of starting something new is just not appealing. There is always the opportunity to make extra income by working a few extra hours each week at work. Or, you may find a second job the solution to reducing your debt.

If you are diligent in your endeavor, and you are consistent with applying every extra dollar earned toward the debt, you will still be better off at the end of the extra work cycle because when you go back to your regular hours, you will have fewer debt payments; you will feel more free in your finances to make choices and have a few extra luxuries you could not afford before. Just be sure not to run up a new bundle of debt by getting too excited about this new freedom. It takes strong resolve to stay on the path once some of the stress has been removed.

Warning! When your income is strong and you have no debt, creditors are willing and ready to give you the "freedom" to buy more. Remember the hard work you put in to get out of debt and refuse to go back.

Let's say you are not into building a business that could provide permanent and potentially passive income. Instead, you want to do some extra work until the debt is paid. There are plenty of options besides getting a second hourly job or adding hours to your current workload. Contract jobs are available that could provide you with pay for the job instead of by the hour. There are virtual assistants offering work all of the time; joining the virtual assistance world may be an easy way for you to use your talents to help others who need to hire out some temporary work.

If you would like to find contract work to add income to your budget to use for repaying debt, some possible opportunities are listed below.

Work a Few Extra Hours Each Month

Again, this is not an exhaustive list; only a few ideas to get your creative mind thinking.

Ideas for extra income:

Ghostwriting: you write content for someone else who publishes it.

Technical work: web-site building, web maintenance, etc.).

Paid research jobs: do the legwork for someone else's research project.

Sell items on eBay or Craigslist.

Find a sales position and earn commission.

Join a multi-level marketing company and promote the product. Note: If you are successful in this business it could become passive income. If you did not want this passive income, you've been warned!

Design marketing campaigns.

Use your talent; create and sell something.

Offer services to your local area that represent your strengths (i.e. painting, decorating, mechanics, etc.)

Create a fundraiser project to reduce your debt. Be sure to carefully disclose the purpose of the project is to reduce your overall debt. Some people may choose to participate because they either want to help you or they want the service or product you are selling.

The Money Makeover

Pause and Reflect

Take inventory of your special talents and gifts you contribute. Once you complete that, jot down how these talents may be able to serve other and earn some extra money for you. Write down everything you think of, no matter how big or small. Remember, writing it down here is just for your information. You are not committing to anything just for writing it down. Once you have discovered your talents and gifts, look up some job offers in your area and see what is being requested in the job market that you could easily offer for a season of time until you reach your goals.

Method 8

Focus on The Percentage

SOMETIMES YOU WANT to reduce a percentage of debt each month. This method is the simplest in context, but one of the more difficult to implement. To use the percentage method, you simply choose the amount of time you would like to spend on reducing debt and calculate the percentage you would need to reduce each month. Then, your payments toward your debt should reflect that amount each month, plus adding the percentage of the highest interest rate as an extra amount to your payment.

For example, let's say the total debt obligation you want to eliminate is $100,000, and your average interest rate is 10%. Your commitment is to be rid of this debt within two years. You would take the $100,000/24 months to get you need to pay each month ($4,167) plus add the amount to cover the interest rate for that month ($100,000 * .10/12 = $833). The total payment of $5,000 each month would have you out of debt within two years.

The Money Makeover

We hope you can see the logic of this method, and be inspired by taking a shorter path to freedom from the burdens of debt

Remember, however, you would most likely combine this payment with the Snowball Method so your average interest rate would decline as you pay off the higher debt. As you can see, this method requires more attention to the resources and to find high cash flow for payments. You can obviously repeat the same activity over a longer period of time to reduce your total debt, and still be successful with this method.

Just so you get a better picture; with the two-year plan, you reduce your debt by about 4% per month. You can also reverse the process: choose a percentage, and calculate the amount of time it will take. To do this, take the percentage you want to eliminate and divide it into 1. If I want to eliminate 5% of my debt per month, I can divide 1 by .05 to get 20 months until the debt is paid. If a smaller payment is all that is possible, you could choose 1-2% of the debt each month.

At 1%, it would take 100 months, or 8.3 years to pay off the debt. The payment for 1% reduction each month on $100,000 would be $1833 ($100,000/100 + $833). Notice the interest

Focus on The Percentage

payment would not change. Each month, however the interest needed would reduce since your total balance is no longer $100,000, and you are therefore no longer paying interest on $100,000. This method works well if you want to put all your resources toward the debt in the early stages (e.g. work for extra money and/or cut back) and have lower payments later so you can stay on target with the lower payments.

For a schedule of what the payments would look like on a two-year plan, see below. Notice how the total payment declines as the balance declines; this is due to less interest owed each month.

Month	Total Debt Owed	Debt Payment
1	$100,000	$5,000
2	$95,833	$4,966
3	$91,666	$4,932
4	$87,499	$4,900
5	$83,332	$4,870
6	$79,165	$4,841
7	$74,998	$4,813
8	$70,831	$4,786
9	$66,664	$4,760
10	$62,497	$4,735
11	$58,330	$4,711

The Money Makeover

12	$54,163	$4,689
13	$49,996	$4,667
14	$45,829	$4,646
15	$41,662	$4,626
16	$37,495	$4,607
17	$33,328	$4,589
18	$29,161	$4,571
19	$24,994	$4,554
20	$20,827	$4,538
21	$16,660	$4,523
22	$12,493	$4,508
23	$8,326	$4,494
24	$4159	$4,480
24	-$0	$4,472

While there are many who wish to pay down the debt using added income, some really want to see the debt disappear... **rapidly**. If you have the resources to do so—and the dedication—the percentage reduction method may be for you. Using the percentage method will pay off your debt rather quickly, but requires some extensive application of your incoming funds for a period of time. While I do not recommend you take on too many "odd jobs" in the long run or commit to paying more on your debt than you can sustain over a longer period of time until it is paid. There are times that you really want to accelerate your

Focus on The Percentage

debt reduction and these options may work to be the catalyst you need to lunge out of debt.

If the percentage method appeals to you but you do not currently have the resources to follow it, you may consider either taking on some extensive extra work or drastically reducing your "fun" spending for a short period of time. Be sure you set a date on this time and stick to the limits so you do not burn out. Somewhere around 3-6 months should be the most you commit at a time toward heavy workloads or extremely strict budgets. After a short break, if so inclined, you could repeat the process again. However, it is not recommended that you sacrifice your well-being to accomplish these goals.

Choose a plan that makes sense for you and stick with that plan. Using this plan, you want to pick a timeline that will allow you to have some form of additional freedom within 12-18 months. If you cannot live the lifestyle that makes you fulfilled after this period of time, choose a longer timeline. There is no shame to take your time to get out of debt. The most important part is being consistent.

The Money Makeover

Pause and Reflect

Take some time to enter your total debt and the percentage of that debt you want to pay down each month. Calculate your percentage and enter it here, or set up an Excel spreadsheet to do the calculations for you. If you need help with this, reach out to us at www.yescrystal.com and let us know where you need support. We can provide the spreadsheet for you.

Percentage to pay down _____

Total Debt _____

Month	Total Debt Owed	Debt Payment
1		
2		
3		
4		
5		
6		
7		
8		
9		
10		
11		
12		
13		

Focus on The Percentage

14		
15		
16		
17		
18		
19		
20		
21		
22		
23		
24		
24		

Method 9

Find Free Money

ONE OF THE most underutilized ways to get out of debt is to search for free assistance. There is frequently money available in the form of grants, scholarships, interest free or low interest loans, and other free money waiting for those who are diligent enough to seek it out. If you have more time than money and no particular trade you have yet learned how to monetize, you may find that to search for the free money sources can become your highway to freedom from debt.

The first thing you want to do to secure free money or interest free money is make a list of all of your own goals, dreams, skills, and potential talents. You can then search for funds that are designed to meet the criteria that match the goals you have listed. Start first with options that are most exiting to you to ensure your proposals will be more authentic. Note: You will be completing a lot of writing for this, so tidy up your writing skills, or find a partner who can write well, and team up to find the possible resources.

Grants are free money given to you for a specific purpose and with no requirements to repay as long as you fulfill your agreement concerning what to do with the funds.

Scholarships are generally offered for some type of achievement and do not need to be repaid. You only need to meet the requirements and be the best applicant among those who also meet the requirements.

Loans will need to be repaid so they do not immediately reduce your debt load but low to no interest loans can alleviate the burden of high interest payments and allow you to focus more on reducing the actual balances of your debt.

There are many resources available on the Internet, but the cheapest and safest sources are found in your public library. Most public libraries have hundreds of books listing available sources of free money. Prepare to take a camera to capture the leads, as you will likely not be able to take these reference books home with you. You can search the listings by type or by whom they serve, what their purpose may be, or many other topics. Using these resources costs nothing monetarily, but finding the rights sources for your needs among the thousands of options will cost a significant amount of time.

There will usually be some essay writing required to get the money as well, so prepare for some essays written specifically to target the purpose of these sources of monies. A crafty way to speed this process a little is to have a template letter that you adjust to meet the guidelines for each new application. While this method is the most cost effective of all methods, you may find you could have better use of your time to find added work during those hours and pay a college student to complete the search, while you earn a higher income during those hours to pay the student, plus bring a little extra home. This is, of course, if you have open opportunities for work at a higher pay grade.

Free money is always the best kind of money, but always remember that your time is also the most expensive resource you have. No amount of money can replace the time once you trade it for something else. Please be sure you use your time for your highest service. For information on how to use your time more profitably and "buy' more

The Money Makeover

time, watch for my future publications on topics like cash flow acceleration and buying time.

Pause and Reflect

To take advantage of this section, first make a list of the talents you have and how each might be used to make a difference in your financial picture. Then, research what sources are available that may offer funds for the special gifts you can bring to the world. Keep in mind, this process can take some time, but it can bring rewards in the form of funds you do not need to repay.

List the address to your local library.

_____
_____
_____
_____
_____
_____
_____
_____

Find Free Money

List special skills you possess, which could be used for improving the world in some way.

_____
_____
_____
_____
_____
_____
_____
_____
_____

Use this space to track the grant offerings you find during your research.

_____
_____
_____
_____
_____
_____
_____
_____
_____
_____
_____
_____

The Money Makeover

Your Next Step

Automate Your Finances

ONE OF THE best things you can do to eliminate debt and stay out of debt permanently is to automate your finances. There are many tools that can assist you in doing this, but you need an overall "system" in order to really eliminate debt and start building wealth. I add this bonus method here so you can understand and take advantage of the value of automation.

There are several steps to automate your financial plan, and I have designed a sound, efficient system to help with that. In this resource, I want to share with you a few easy tips to automate your finances and reduce debt... and then I will show you how you can take advantage of other available resources to expand the process—with additional help.

The first tip to automate your finances is to use the resources provided by your bank. You need to have more than one bank account; I recommend three with at least two different banks in the mix.

First you go through the process of tracking and having a clear picture of your income and regular monthly bills. You are then going to arrange for the amount needed to cover your bills each month to automatically deposit into the account you use to pay them.

If you are an employee, your employer will likely send a portion of your pay to the account for you. If not, you can arrange for your bank to automatically transfer the additional funds to another account. If you are in business for yourself or your pay is not regular, you will arrange for the first amount to go to your "bill pay" account and the remainder to be placed in your other account(s).

Next you are going to set up all of your monthly payments to automatically be withdrawn directly to the recipient. Some recipients will even give you a discount or a percentage reduction on the debt for automatic payments.

For recipients who cannot automatically withdraw funds, most banks will set up payments for you and send the checks on the same day each month directly from your account. Once you know all of your monthly bills are automatically paid, you will immediately start to feel wealthier... just by eliminating the stress of worrying over bills being timely paid.

More importantly, automation helps many people avoid painful late charges due to forgotten payments and—add the value of the late payment to their net worth—on the spot. Don't forget to include in your bill-pay account the monthly amount you have selected from your budget to focus on debt reduction.

The next question is what do you do with the remainder of your money. Now, look back over your spending history and determine how much you need for entertainment, food, clothing, and other items that are not the same each month. You will send a portion of your money to the second account and call it your spending account. Each month you can choose where you spend the money.

If dining out is more important to you than a new outfit that month, use some of your clothing money for dining out. If you have an important date or event, clothing may be more important to you some months. This is a flexible account; you can spend all of it every month if you so choose, or save for something on which you want to spend more.

You have created an immediate sense of satisfaction by adding more choice to your life.

All you need to do is know the available balance in this account so you do not go over your available funds, and you can have fun and buy anything you have made a conscious choices about wanting.

Now let's talk about that third account. What I want to encourage you to do is eventually set a goal of sending at least 20% of your income to this third account. If you cannot afford 20% up front, start with a small percentage like 1-2% and over time work increase that proportion as your income increases or other obligations decrease. This fund is your savings.

You can choose to break your accounts down further if you wish. Look for banks that offer free checking or savings accounts so you can have as many as you need. The savings portion of your income can be focused strictly on debt reduction while you are in this stage financially, but as you make progress, you can designate the funds for other desires such as travel, large purchases, and other luxuries. Be sure to also make some room in your budget to save for what I call an *opportunity fund.*

An Opportunity Fund™ is money you put away in a safe account—safe from your fingers—so that when a sudden, unexpected, amazing opportunity comes your way you are prepared with cash "in hand" to take advantage of the occasion.

Pause and Reflect

Now is the time to choose. You have seen more than nine strategies to reduce your debt and increase your income. It is time to choose which method or methods you will begin to use and how. List the top three methods that most appealed to you while reading. Choose one or two of them and write out a daily action plan.

The Money Makeover

Which methods appealed to you most?

_____
_____
_____
_____
_____
_____
_____
_____
_____

Why did these methods appeal to you?

_____
_____
_____
_____
_____
_____
_____
_____
_____
_____
_____
_____

Your Next Step

Which top one or two will you choose to implement first?

_____
_____
_____
_____
_____
_____
_____
_____
_____

How will you incorporate those strategies into your life?

_____
_____
_____
_____
_____
_____
_____
_____
_____
_____

The Money Makeover

Write out three action steps you will take to start implementing your plan right away.

_____
_____
_____
_____
_____
_____
_____
_____
_____
_____

What is your timeline to implement these steps?

_____
_____
_____
_____
_____
_____
_____
_____
_____
_____
_____
_____

Your Next Step

Once you have completed each step, come back and repeat this exercise again; choosing three more action steps each time until this plan is fully implemented. Then, you may wish to go back through the strategies and add yet another!

Follow Through
Work Your Plan

ONCE YOU HAVE all the right *system* in place, it is important to create a plan to help you follow through and implement the pieces you have included in that system. There are three primary ways discussed here, which can magnify your chances of follow-through on your dream of living debt free.

First, you need to **create a buddy system** to have an accountability partner. Second, you want to enlist some type of supportive competition to motivate you to stay on track, and finally you need to have a plan for positive reinforcement and rewards.

Let's talk first about a buddy system. Using one creates a mode of accountability so you can be supported through those times you would typically give up on your plan. Select a friend, family member, or other accountability partner carefully; they need to be as committed to their goal as you are committed to yours.

If you do not have access to an accountability partner, you can contact your local credit union, which usually offers support programs for members who want to reduce debt or reach other financial goals. You will need to create a plan for checking in with each other, such as weekly, to report your progress toward the goals you set, and to discuss those you did not reach and what seemed to be your blocks or reasons for not reaching your goals.

If you need support in a particular area, your buddy can help with the motivation and keep you moving along. It could be that you do not have the proper systems or plans to implement those goals and your support team may be able to help you craft the proper plan to meet your needs in moving forward. If you still feel like you are not making progress or are not supported like you would like to be, consider hiring a financial coach to guide you through the efforts required.

You can contact our financial coaches by visiting us at www.crystalgifford.com and filling out our contact form, explaining your coaching needs. You may also apply for a strategy session to determine your needs at www.yescrystal.com.

Your Next Step

The next thing you will want to do is create a system of supportive competition. You can set some specific goals and timelines and create a competition either with yourself or with a partner or group so you have a measurement against which you can work to accomplish your goal of eliminating debt. Competition creates a more passionate sense of necessity to complete your goals and helps create a timeline to help keep you on track.

Don't forget to make this part of debt reduction fun and competitive even if you are doing it alone; "work it" with others who have similar goals. The more fun you make this, and the more competitive you can be... the more you will discover you actually have the staying power to get the work done, which is necessary to reach your goals.

Finally, you must develop a system of positive reinforcement and rewards to enjoy along your journey to debt-free living. Positive reinforcement may come in the form of revisiting your financial statements monthly to see the difference it has made to reduce your debt so your decisions continue to stay focused on your goal.

The Money Makeover

The necessary positive reinforcement can also come in the form of finding encouragement or acknowledgement from your current support system; someone to let you know you are on the right track and inspire you to keep moving forward. You will also want a reward system to efficiently and effectively encourage better spending behaviors through your desire for immediate and short-term rewards.

Using the Steps!

NOW THAT YOU have access to the top ways to reduce debt, it is important to follow the strategic steps that allow you to properly implement those debt reduction strategies you choose. The steps are outlined below:

Steps to Using the Methods:

Step 1:	Create a healthy relationship with money.
Step 2:	Select 2-3 methods you will use to start; no more than this to avoid overwhelm.
Step 3:	Find an accountability partner and consistently apply the methods for no less than three months.
Step 4:	Assess the outcome and how you feel.
Step 5:	Evaluate your methods and continue or select other methods to replace or add to the mix you chose.

The Money Makeover

Step 6:	Celebrate your successes and forgive the failures.
Step 7:	Repeat the cycle.

For additional help with these steps, fill out your application for a free consultation at www.yescrystal.com.

Why Debt Can Be Wonderful

UNTIL NOW WE have focused on how you can eliminate debt, but there are some types of debt that can be quite useful; countering the type of debt that can bring financial ruin. Let's take a moment to distinguish the two. The first, "evil" debt is called consumer debt. This is debt that accumulates in the pursuit of "stuff" that neither builds value for the future nor contributes to future income.

While I am a strong advocate of living life to its fullest potential and enjoying your money now, there are some clear guidelines you need to understand and follow to make this kind of debt a long-term, sustainable part of your life plan. The first thing you need to understand is that you must distinguish between choosing the luxuries you want—that your current income can provide—and the luxuries for which you need to save and prepare to enjoy.

Consumer goods don't have to be a guilt-indulgence part of life... they should be enjoyed.

The Money Makeover

What you must understand, however, is that using debt for consumer goods creates more frustration and stress in the long term than the reward offered in the short term. The use of consumer debt is not suggested as a proper use of your resources. Consumer debt is very likely exactly what brought you to a place where you need to get out of the debt you may be in right now.

I want you to enjoy all the luxuries life has to offer, but I want you to be able to do it not only today, but for tomorrow and the remaining years of your life. Therefore, consumer debt is not always the proper or best use of your funds. Keep in mind, this does not mean you cannot buy consumer goods. My instructions are that the purchase of consumer goods be reserved for the cash you have available as *free cash flow* in your overall financial plan, and that you make conscious decisions about when and where you spend on consumer goods. For help with this, contact us at www.crystalgifford.com to make an appointment.

About the Author

Enough about consumer debt! I promised you I would show you how debt **can** be good. So let's start with why debt is wonderful and how you can use it to make millions. The second type of debt (good debt) is investment debt. This is the type of debt you take on that you can at least utilize its power to create new value (assets) or generate future income in the form of added cash flow. These investments are often referred to as capital investments.

Some activities, programs, and products have the power to generate more than their initial cost, and can contribute to growing your net worth and capacity to enjoy even more luxuries in the future. If you are looking for a way to build a lifestyle of luxury, it is imperative you make this distinction and use debt only when the purchase or expenditure clearly contributes to an expanded financial future.

To clarify this discussion, we will conclude with some examples of spending that would be classified as consumer spending and those which would be classified as capital spending. As you review the following chart, stop and think about recent purchases you may have made, and determine which category into which they would fit, and whether you would now make those same purchases.

Consumer spending (AKA bad debt)	Capital spending (AKA good debt)	Mixed spending (Depends on use)
Clothing	Equipment	Cars
Vacations	Real estate	Jewelry
Dining out	Business Investments	Homes
Electronics	Business Operation Needs (Start Up)	Personal Development
Latest trendy items	Travel for Business, Events, or Education	Technology

While some of these examples are clearly not good uses of debt, others can be viewed as the perfect opportunity to incorporate leverage, and make a difference in your ability to reach your business goals. Some expenditures; however, are in the "mixed" category because the results for use of debt for these depends on their ultimate use.

For instance, a car you use to drive to work and allows you to earn income could be justified

About the Author

for taking on debt to acquire it. Jewelry and homes may appreciate in value, but you must recognize that these are not guaranteed to do so. Use of debt for these should be treated carefully. Many people are unaware it is now easy to complete an analysis to determine if renting or buying a home is the best investment.

Additionally, consider the possibility you might have fallen into a trap, and become a personal development "junkie" like some of us are. Even when you make an investment in personal development, you should stop first to evaluate the return you have gained in the past. Used properly, personal development can be a good opportunity for leverage to launch your business to new levels of income that will more than pay for your investment over time. The important key is to know, which is why our application remains open to you for any support you may need at www.yescrystal.com.

All in all, the use of debt has its place in your life, especially business. However, remember that when you allow debt to be improperly used, it can easily lead to stress, overwhelm, shame, and even depression. The purpose of this book is to shed a light on what debt represents in your life and help you overcome any strongholds debt may have on your well-being.

While we do not expect you to follow all of the methods in this book at one time, or even all of them at any given time, it is suggested you select those that appeal most to you and use them to achieve your goals. The good news is, if you identify with even one of these methods, which you will consistently apply, you are on the right path to being debt free.

One final thought... I mentioned to you earlier that we would address the concept of budget and teach you how to make this a less "constricting word." I want you to understand that a budget is a tool. Used in conjunction with these strategies, a budget simply informs you of where your money is so you can make better choices.

The key word here is "choice." You can choose not to use a budget and be constrained for life, or you can choose to use one and ultimately be free to make better choices, and draw on the information you are now armed with to make them. At the end of the day—you choose.

We are here to support you in your journey to eliminate harmful debt from your life and build

About the Author

abundance. Our programs work with purpose-driven entrepreneurs, like you, to guide you to a guilt-free, sustainable life of luxury. This is your first step to luxurious living. Live abundantly and be blessed.

References

The information in this eBook is written exclusively from the expertise and experience of Dr. Crystal Dawn Gifford, CFP®

You were provided different "connection" points throughout the book. They are repeated here for your convenience:

crystal@crystalgifford.com

www.crystalgifford.com

www.empoweredgift.com

www.financialdevelopment.org

www.yescrystal.com

Before you go, you owe it to yourself to gain access to my five secrets to turning you cash flow into abundant wealth today at

www.empoweredgift.com

About the Author

A FEATURED AUTHOR in the international best selling book, *The Live Sassy Formula,* and in *CFO Magazine*, Dr. Crystal D. Gifford, CFP guides professional athletes and six-figure entrepreneurs using her Massive Revenue Strategy™ for their business and their lives. Her dedication to help others create the financial freedom that comes from designing income streams, which pay indefinitely for their expertise, has earned Crystal recognition both in financial and business circles across the globe.

If you are ready to take your dream life to the next level, and you are tired of being told you have to "sacrifice" now for a good future later, you are in for a treat. Dr. Crystal D. Gifford, CFP® is known for her extensive expertise and spot on remedies for healthy financial living and worry-free wealth. For over 15 years she has helped clients maximize the impact of their success and live their dreams and luxury lifestyles through financial development and efficient resource planning, Dr. Gifford brings the difficult and often taboo topic of finances to clients in an easy-to-understand, applicable format.

Standing tall as a visionary leader, Crystal's clients have said that she has a unique ability to help them see their own strengths, which then gives them the courage to create grand visions for their lives. Her work has helped thousands craft a plan to manifest those dreams into reality. Her indisputable talents to authentically see the silver lining in clients' circumstances has brought clients to study with Dr. Gifford from all over the world. It has often been said Dr. Gifford has an "optimism that brightens even the darkest of rooms."

Dr. Gifford's philosophy is that money matters should be fun and uplifting, and her approach supports this philosophy. For those of you who seek to create massive revenue streams that last a lifetime, Dr. Gifford has the tools you need to harness the power of your prosperity.

About the Author

In just two short years following a divorce, and as a single mother with two sons, Crystal created a six-figure income from her expertise in financial planning and education. She quickly learned that creating this income had to come with life balance, if she was going to be a good mother to her boys. After her first six-figure year, Crystal found a system that would allow the income to keep coming and generate plenty of time for her family. She then grew her income by 100% within two years and took numerous vacations and time off with her boys.

During this time, serving as a professor at an HBCU, Crystal worked with athletes in her classes, some of whom were heading into the pros. Witnessing the financial dangers they faced as the market began to consume student athletes, she found great joy in helping them create a plan to remain financially successful as they entered their sport. This experience led Dr. Gifford to establish The International Center for Athletic Financial Development™ to guide college and professional athletes to powerful financial strategies that allow them to fully enjoy their earnings both now and in the future.

The Money Makeover

To book Dr. Gifford as a speaker for your group, or for more resources, tools, and tips, visit www.financialdevelopment.org and enter your contact information so you may stay up to date with her latest releases.

About the Author

Crystal Offers Solutions to:

1. A path to financial freedom.

2. A guilt-free, sustainable life of luxury.

3. The onramps to bringing dreams into reality and sustaining that dream.

4. Overcome the overwhelm that often comes with money matters.

5. Build your income while saving you time.

6. Live the life you thought you could only dream of living without breaking the bank.

7. Making the Big Time Last a Lifetime—for high-income earners who want to make sure success lasts.

A complimentary luxurious living consultation awaits you at www.yescrystal.com

Thank you!

...for reading *The Money Makeover*. We trust you have not only enjoyed these rich possibilities for building a better relationship with your finances and learning to be debt free, and will find some of them inspired you to find a different perspective on your own life and financial decisions. Thank you in advance for taking the time to post a review for the book on Amazon; many readers will not take that "step" to purchase and read… until they know someone else has "led" the way.

http://amzn.to/1EuCzD1

Do you have friends, family or professional peers who prefer digital format? The Money Makeover is also available in digital format! on Kindle:

http://www.amazon.com/dp/B00C3HKMUQ

About the Author

Other Books By Dr. Gifford

{An} Unsinkable Soul: The Phoenix Lives Again

Quite frankly... life happens! In {An} Unsinkable Soul readers will find stories by purpose-directed authors who have learned to bounce back from life's challenges, creating Unsinkable concepts they have come to live... as dynamic and transformational experts who want to lead others to a better place in what we call LIFE! {An} Unsinkable Soul was written to provide and encourage readers to look differently at life challenges, and in bouncing back from them... to continue moving forward. At the end of the day, readers will find hope and love in the midst of chaos and uncertainty.

http://www.amazon.com/dp/0615970176

Live Sassy Formula: **Make Big Money and a Big Difference Doing What You Love!**

You know in your heart... there's a bigger plan for your life

http://www.amazon.com/dp/B00DIL0KDK

The Money Makeover

Coming Soon

"The Money Shot: The Professional Athlete's Financial Playbook to Make the Big Time last a Lifetime"

NOTES:

The Money Makeover

Notes

The Money Makeover

Notes

The Money Makeover

Notes

The Money Makeover

Notes

The Money Makeover

www.ingramcontent.com/pod-product-compliance
Lightning Source LLC
Chambersburg PA
CBHW071954070426
42453CB00008BA/704